all of her love

Alexandra Heather Foss

First Printed 2022

ISBN: 978-1-957789-01-9

Author Website: www.alexandraheatherfoss.com
Author Instagram: @allofherworld
Author Photography: @withlovefromcapecod

DEDICATION

For my beloved mother, who defines for me, love.

Your love is like the sun. I love you always.

ACKNOWLEDGMENTS

Aside from my mother, father, son, and grandparents, who are always deserving of love, and thanks, there are a number of intimate others worth acknowledging here. There isn't the space to do each person justice, but at different times in my life, these people have been significant parts of my story. They are in my heart because of what at one time we have shared.

My brother, William, was my first friend. As a child, I didn't have many friends. In fact, I never have. For different reasons, at different times, but mostly because I do better one-on-one. But my baby brother and I had many adventures together. We played on Cape Cod beaches, and rocks in Maine, we swam in Florida pools, and admired changing leaves in Vermont, and for all the days and nights growing up in New York, he was a favorite part. We built snow igloos, we watched movie marathons, and for every holiday and meal he was there. The sibling relationship is unique. We are the only two people to share a foundation, and though we now are adults, geographically distant, both with busy lives, and families of our own, we will always have that shared beginning, and everything that was a part of that.

For the love and care she offers me, my son, and my family, Fatima deserves special thanks. Her warm heart is a weekly reminder there are kind and nurturing people in this world. When I am sick, she brings me homemade yuca soup, and her garlic rice nourishes more than my son's body. She has been like an aunt to me, since I was a girl, and I am grateful my son Oliver has her as such a solid part of his foundation.

My friend Maura has been with me to pick out Christmas trees, during Thanksgivings, in college and after. She flew up multiple times, after my romantic relationship ended, to give me something to look forward to, and every Italian, French, and Chinese meal we share includes much more than food and drink. I have often gone to her for advice, and comfort. I value our memories.

Fiona reminds me with her letters and love a sister can be someone across a sea, unrelated by blood. I had been looking for her friendship, long before we met, and I feel understood on a soul level, every time we connect. She is one of the major reasons I feel happiness. I feel lucky to have found her.

My spiritual awareness and intellectual functioning are expanded by the conversations I have with my friend Stephanie. She is sensitive, smart, deep, and artistic. We share history, a love of nature, she is warm to my son, and her input and wisdom have been instrumental at key times in my life. She is another kindred spirit.

And Andrea has been a gentle presence in my life since we were younger than my son. The sweet gifts she sends for special occasions, the times we watched *Star Wars* in her house while her grandmother made yummy smelling things upstairs, our shared childhood birthdays, all of it matters to me. She was the first friend I made my age, and she will always be important.

Other loved ones I am thankful for include Vicky, my little Fiona, Ducky, Beary, Elaine for the years of involvement and love that have been a core part of my son's life, as well as mine, Polly, Maestro, Buttercup, Zodiac, Winston, Aunt Gerry, Thea, Reddie, Freddie, Vera, Joyce, my sister-in-law Stephanie, and sweet nephew James, my niece, Harriet, Clayton, and Delilah, everyone who is part of my ancestral heritage, and all the other non-human animal family members we have had.

Louise, Janice, the Paynes, Jen, Julia, Toni, the Godomskis, Lizbeth, Katerina, members of my Thursday matinée CLOC crew, including Ursula, the Cronigs, Marcia, Jamie, Jane, Norman, and Lloyd, my Rollins College alums, my Long Beach lovers, and letter writers, everyone at Salerno's, Asia, and the other restaurants we have loved, old friends, and newer friends, like Amanda, Meghan, and their children, I care about you all.

And then the two men, who have inspired so many of these words, who are known on allofherworld, as Jack, and Angelo. Romantic relationships, for me, come closest to family, because of the level of intimacy. To share of oneself that way requires a safety, and comfort, that in my experience rarely happens. Even if all we have now is confined to the past, what I will take with me into my present, and future, from knowing these men, will shape my life always.

The relationship I shared with Jon, from our late teens to mid-thirties, that for me was like a marriage, taught me more about myself and life than almost anything. Because I felt seen by him, loved, and safe, I was able to grow mentally, emotionally, and spiritually. Our relationship is one of the most special I will have. We were college sweethearts, we explored the world together, we shared homes, and families, we laughed. That sacred time for me was fun, and beautiful, sweet, and tender. Life may have divided us, but he is someone I will love. As will I be grateful for our rich history. I am who I am today largely because of the us we created together. I miss him. He was my dear friend, and partner.

And Angelo, my rainbow in the storm. Before this book was divided into three parts, that was the title. *Rainbow in the Storm.* Which, for me, was him. Rainbows are the gifts storms give us, magical displays of color, and hope. When I drove to meet Angelo the first time, it was like I was driving through a hurricane, tsunami, and tornado. My life was a storm that wouldn't break. But when he took my hand, my skies cleared, and all I could see were strokes of luminous color. Everywhere there were rainbows.

For years, I have tried to capture in words his impact, and I am not sure I will ever be able to do it. Angelo saved my life. That isn't why I love him, but that is why he is one of the people I am most grateful for. The path he walked me down, that looked from the outside like it was made just of water, trees, sky, and concrete, has led me to so many beautiful things. Things that could only come from knowing him.

Sometimes we meet someone and we are changed. That happens, of course, from every interaction we have with others, the butterfly effect of social connection is profound, but micro shifts aren't what I am referring to here. A mother, a father, a son, a lover, certain people shift us in dramatic ways, like switches, for trains on a track. The track we continue on, after that moment of meeting, whether that moment be a birth, or a walk by a canal, is fundamentally different from the one we were previously travelling. And we are substantially more.

Angelo was the path that led me to motherhood, to my son, to sharing my writing and photography with others, to trails I have walked with Oliver, to unparalleled passion, and an awareness of my personal power. Everything that has happened since October of 2016 has happened in some way because I met him. With him I had peace. I felt certain, and alive. He was a breath of fresh air. An angel without wings. Someone who filled me with life, poetry, a renewed sense of purpose, and meaning, as well as the future that is now my present. Our time may have been brief, but my feelings for him are eternal. There will always be stars in my heart, shining only for him.

There has been Cape Cod, Florida, New York, and Maine. I have been shaped by villages and sacred spots in those states, such as Long Beach, Schoodic, Fort Hill, and Bolen Bluff trail. There have been Caribbean islands and European cities, the Eiffel tower, the Cinque Terre, the Space Needle, Ravello, Cotuit, Sint Maarten, and Bermuda caves. I am grateful to places around the world, that have nourished me, and educated me, with culture, and opportunity, as strangers have become friends, digitally, and in person.

There have been books, and meals, home-cooked and prepared out, Chinese take-out, piano music, pajamas, tubs, handbells, nature trails, board games, musical theater, unicorns, dinosaurs, stuffed animals, holidays, Disney, flowers and sunshine. Thank you to color and garden herbs, art and meaning, as well as the moon, the sun, and everything below and in between. And for anyone or thing not included here in writing, out of either oversight, or space, you still are a part of me, and I am grateful.

And thank you again to every reader and supporter of allofherworld, and now these books. These exist, because you believe in these words, and I am lucky that you do.

PREFACE

I decided to break the hundreds of allofherworld posts into three books because having them together was too crowded. When I was considering what topics to focus on, it just felt natural to have pain, which is what started this writing story, healing, which is what I have been doing ever since (hopefully), and love.

Love isn't an easy concept or practice. It is a basic need, I have learned even more so, from being a parent. Something as essential as food, water, shelter, and air. We need love to develop, feel safe, and grow, in happy and healthy ways. That is how we flourish. With the love we receive from others, as well as the love that we give to others. But it also isn't as simple as that, as likely every adult, and probably many children, sadly knows.

In some ways I have been lucky in love. With family, friendships, and romantic relationships. I have had parents and grandparents who love me, a son, a long partnership. But I also have been challenged. Some of the love I have known has been reciprocal, but not all of it, and so this book is also a little bit about pain. Which, of course, life is. There is always a mix.

I have learned through the years that you can absolutely love someone, in a true and lasting way, without them offering love in return. Unconditional love is a real thing, even if sometimes we wish it wasn't. But that doesn't mean it doesn't hurt, to love alone, that it doesn't take something from us, we may never be able to get back. A trust, or belief in enchantment.

I write daily about love because that is what my heart feels, and I have learned on this account that the only way for me to write, in a way that others connect with, including myself, is by accessing both heart and soul, with as much raw truth as I can. Hundreds of posts I have written about people who were actively in my life once, but not necessarily now, and yet that doesn't mean they aren't still always with me, just in a different form than I might wish.

My mother has often said that "happiness has no history," and I think what she means by that is that when things are good, we might not think to necessarily say so, because we are overall happy, and resolved. It is when the living become ghosts, as I once wrote, but we are the ones with the unfinished business, manifesting itself in the form of longing and memory, when there is on some levels more to say.

If I had romantic love, if I were wanted too, would I have this same daily pull, to extract from within me these unspent loving words? I didn't write much about love when I was in a loving romantic relationship. I wrote more about nature, the Universe, and relationships, yes, but in the context of conflicts that would arise, likely because that was my unfinished business then. Are these words like a toll I pay, so that I can go on with my day? Things I wish I could say in person, but can't? I am not sure.

I think we tend to emphasize things in life that are missing, or aren't right in some way. Not to be negative, or delusional, in the case of unrequited love, but because that is what we can't figure out, or even out, within ourselves. I think we seek to resolve, whether it is sharing our words online, or during a conversation with a friend or family member, whatever it is that doesn't make sense to us. The confounding, and the incomprehensible.

I like reading these words, this winding love poem broken into smaller bits, because they are a tribute to my heart, as much as anything. Yes, how I long to be again inside certain arms, to feel a heart beating against my chest that isn't my own, to experience intimacy. I miss being comfortable inside a relationship that felt like it would never go anywhere, I miss making meals, and going to food and wine festivals, having someone to talk with about our days, and feelings, having someone to kiss in the morning and night, someone to laugh with. But love is with me, as these words show, a part of me, regardless of any external circumstances. I am alone but not, because of how my heart works. That it works.

To be romantic, to be loving, and open, is to say grace is here inside me, as is the magic inherent within all life. I am proud I can still do that. That, instead of closing, I opened further than I ever had. Every day that goes by, where it is love that more fills my heart, than any negative form of emotion, I consider a personal triumph.

Being a loving person is not a weakness. Loving others, wholly, is not a weakness. It may feel like that, during lonely nights and days, but it is a sign of courage and strength, to be able to emphasize love within, and without, when so much of life is hard.

I am grateful that beautiful words and feelings have come into my life because love has existed for me, at the least, in my own heart. And for the people, here still, or gone, who in direct and indirect ways have allowed me to feel as I do, feel as I might not otherwise have without them, I am lucky.

And so this is my tribute to love, presented in a way that made sense to me while compiling it. I hope while you are reading, you are reminded of the people in your life, who fill your heart, as my people, fill mine.

The magic of love lives in all of us.

Mom

So often in my life,
I feel lost in translation.
I fight out of fright,
or flee into a sliver of a self
I would not recognize
to see on the street.
I hug you and I feel
I belong in this world,
you my ultimate witness,
the home made of skin,
that even in absence
stands by my side.
Your smile could warm the sun.
Your eyes are the earth
always beneath my feet,
your heart the melody
of my favorite song.
With you, days open
like flowers eager to bloom,
and like your hair,
nights glitter with stars.
Mother is a word
with many meanings,
but you define it as
a constant source of love,
and the reason we all are here.

The Resurrection
(or the Story of How You Came to Be)

The memory of you
fades into the skin of another.
I forget who I am meant to love,
as he and I become one
inside the starlight of a forgotten wood.

I thought never could I want
like I wanted for so long you,
until, his electric touch
shocked the sadness
from my tortured mind
recharging my flat-lined heart.
A coup de foudre in the storm
of our destruction.

He wends,
like a coiled strand of DNA
defining the essential fabric
of my earthly fantasies,
curling desires
underneath my thoughts,
until all I breathe,
is all I want with him.

I inhale him, he, the air
of my resurrection.
Our primal dance,
soft but also strong,
flows like water,
a river of sweat and tears.

I thought no soul had known my pain,
until he confessed
the same desperate wish.

Perhaps it was then I knew
he had the power
to bend my destiny.

Words he spoke,
full of buried longing,
deeply penetrated
the part of me
I thought had died with us.
He breathed new life
into my ashes,
and the shape forged
under his command
looked more like me,
and less like you.

Into him I was pulled,
he rapt me in his touch,
tall, with hands rough,
and eyes molten,
all parts of him
felt strangely familiar
to all parts of me.

And for once.
I simply trusted.
That maybe not everything is a lie.
That perhaps flowers can grow
from the bones of broken truths.

His fertile kisses promise,
solid as his body against mine,
the children that we never had.
And for the first time,
since your breaking glance,
he releases hope
inside of me, and I realize,
I have never wanted anything more.

Uncensored Poetry

Rattle my soul. Be kind but not gentle. I want to feel, like moonlight spinning in a jar, still, yet filled entirely with kinetic light. I want your words to move me, raw and real, uncensored poetry spilling from your page, unfinished, like the unpolished heartbeat of a new lover. Be my lover. Be my friend. Unravel my tight, twisted knots. Say yes. Mean it. Mean every second we share. Handle me with an intensity that matches mine. Promise me never will I be too much, can't be, show me you want more. The sweet honey, combing like a river, through my grand canyons, open me wide, color me in the fiery light of dawn. Paint your soul on my skin, my lips, I want the name I taste in my fantasies to be yours. Shelter the soft tears that shed my sorrows. Do not turn them away. Embrace all of me, like there is no other choice, on your heart tattoo my name, in indelible ink, and I will do the same, so that even when our bones consume our flesh, we will remain.

Like Candy
(A Valentine's Wish)

be you

if I wanted another
to wrap me like candy
in their arms
and bite into
my surprise center
I would be kissing
their lips

be mine

When We Were We

I felt safe
to be the me
that others
do not see
when we
were we.

Moonlit Mount

Side by side
we ascended
that moonlit mount
into a sky
with stars the shape
of fireflies.

In Creamy Pools

You collect
in creamy pools
of light
on our back porch
a scalloped shell
a tiny twig
the sound
your smile makes
when you clap
the feel
of the wind as
you lift yourself up
life new
for you
abundant
and wise.

I collect
these memories
like sacred jewels
the color of
your eyes.

A Future

you are
the reason
I have
a future

So Close

You came close
within reach
your lips
your breath that
had given me
new life
new love
I wanted
to kiss you
take your hand
your heart
feel your cheek
next to mine
keep you safe
loved
you have never
been loved right
your hands
in my hair
on my hips
my belly
feeling
the life we made
made for
each other
I wanted
to hold you
longer
than our last
embrace
deeper
love you
more than
a memory
all of you
always
all ways

Oasis

Every footstep
I have taken

walked me
in your direction.

You were the oasis
in my desert.

Always

there has not been,
since I met you,
a moment when I
have not loved you

I Can't Forget That Love

your body sang melodies
that echo deeper than skin
I can't forget that love
where the end came before the beginning
because my whole life led me there
back to the home of your heart
all the stories time could have told
if given by you the chance

Forever With You

together meant forever
when I was with you

Love

Love is the heart of life
that beats between breaths.
Love also is the loss
that almost kills us.

Love is the sun
forever untouched
who in that cold truth
chooses to be warm.

Love is the wasp
who builds a home
for its family
during a hurricane.

Love is the giant sea turtle
in a rigged carnival game
he always tried
to win me.

Love is my mother
holding my baby
beside me
in a womblike sea.

Love is the purpose.
Love is the meaning.
Love is the answer.
Love is the question.

Love wraps around eternity
like a newborn child's finger
and even when it breaks
it fills itself with gold.

My Love

If my love were a star,
it would be the sun.

What I Remember

There was a lecture
but what I remember
is the smell of vanilla
cream and yeast
rising in peaks
like smoke from a
slow churning barbecue
the evening train
making its way
down the tracks
like an old man
how your eyes
green as fanning palms
smiled with your lips
as you gathered
fallow oranges
from ground fertile
with passion flowers
and runaway vines.

My Little Eternity

you reach
through spindles
in my wooden chair
a hand
that never
has harmed anyone
blessed I am
you reach for me
touching my life
with your love
my little
eternity

Oliver

Held first by womb
and forever in heart

Captive

my heart
is captive
to your beat

Choosing You

choosing you was easy
you are not perfect
nor are you for me
what I deserve
but I was sure
the way rock
knows to be solid
and water to flow
that for a lifetime
I could be yours

Breath of Fresh Air

there was no air left
only stale lifeless thoughts
through hundreds I swiped
each one not him so I pled
in desperate midnight moments
for the one for me truly meant
you hid behind another face
but still I saw you in words
that dove into my heart
loving you felt like breathing
instinctual and organic
not because you are an angel
although for me you were
but because in your arms
I felt like I belonged

Autumn and Everything After

you are the fire
that lights the trees from within
I was okay with summer dying
when you were by my side
I am here
if ever you feel cold

The Heart Outside My Chest

my heart beats for you
as if we still were one

The Alchemy of Being

I breathed in
and you were one
last year we were
seconds precious
as prized stones
slip sideways
into the seasons
oak leaves edging
into persimmon
and wild mulberry
shedding their
summer clothes
and in the quiet
echo of light
from our kitchen pane
you explore the
alchemy of being
as with two feet
you rise and
walk to me

A Woman Loves

A woman loves
when only shadows
taste her skin,
when browning petals
take their final descent,
when to the heart
she becomes ashes.
A woman loves
because she is
fire and forgiveness,
she blossoms after being
ripped from the earth,
her wild call rides the tides
of the wind like a seed,
that remembers the
first cradle of life
that welcomed her
into the womb of time.
A woman loves
because her resilience
is forged with
tectonic force,
only does she succumb
when she wants to be won.
A woman loves
in the ephemeral space
that so briefly makes a life
because she knows
hate is wasted treasure.

Photograph

life before you
was like a black and white photograph.
I could see,
just not in color.

Eternal Bond

there will never be a period for me
at the end of our sentence

My Purple Florida Typewriter

I was not the first to have you
many stories you wrote without me
but together we make poetry
and though my love came later
with you I could write into forever

Voice Box

the heart
is the
voice box
for the soul

Wishful Hours

My hand longs for your hand.
My heart for your heart.
In these wishful hours
that slip from the years,
love no longer makes sense
the way it once did,
where pieces fit together,
in orderly ways.
This feeling is more like stars
scattered across a space,
galaxies long, and an eternity wide.
Maybe we were only a dream,
and that is what we will stay,
but together still never felt better
than when I was with you.

Held

he held me the way
a dream holds the night

Eternal Knowing

My feet feel the ground
even with my eyes closed,
and melodies stay the same
in every language.
Whether I see the sun
serenade the horizon
with chords of color,
it still is there,
as is the moon
punctuating night.
Love is not a fickle
arrangement of letters,
or a lottery of appearance.
It is an eternal knowing,
and a steady hand,
that says no matter
how today you choose to be,
or who you hide behind,
my heart is yours.

When You Truly Know

It might have been
for a short time,
a long time ago,
but it only
takes a second,
when you truly know.

Angels and Devils

I liked that with you
not only our angels
came out to play
but our devils too.

The Heart That Beat Within My Walls

I had only imagined you
the ears you would hear birdsong with
the eyes that would view mountains
we met first in darkness
you the heart that beat within my walls
and when you came into the light
every past step made sense

The One She Needed

she looked at him
like maybe he was the one
not the one long ago she had
or who as a girl she imagined
but the one she needed
to take her into his heart
and keep her there

A Thousand Tomorrows

for one more night with you
I would trade a thousand tomorrows
with someone new

Made For

I wait,
because I remember
what it felt like
to be made for someone.

Passion

passion had
always been
an idea,
not a person,
before I met you.

When you smile, all the happiness
I have had in this life smiles too.
That backyard robin that brightly sang
into trees tufted with onion grass,
the ivory scent of melodies played
by the nurturing hands of my mother,
how gently the cradle of a soft
summertime day offered me shelter.

The moments dipped in afterglow
reminded me when all felt lost
that tucked within a tender heart,
however wholly breaking, is love
for times that do not change their mind.

You are here because I had hope
hungrier than my heartbreak,
that somewhere in the shadows
stood someone sturdier than a dream.

You are the heart of heaven
and how lucky am I to be your mother.

Homesick

you were the home,
I did not know
I was sick for.

Because You Exist

had you not been born
green would be just a color
the world outlines on a map
I grew into myself by your side
and with you love became a verb
so much of what I know now
I learned because you exist

The Only Answer

a lifetime she asked questions
about God and dreams and space
where her feet should lead her
who to walk with on the way
the wheel of thought spun
her into weary submission
until a stranger appeared
like the only answer
to the only question
she ever wanted to know
he had holes in his shirt
and eyes like fireworks
and of her he asked nothing
but simply took her hand
and opened the door
carrying her away
from all confusion

Tomorrow May

tomorrow may bring
what today seems impossible

Deep Inside Me

it was a line of text
a couple steps
a short drive away
I was unprepared for you
for how deep inside me
you would go
and now you live here
in my heart
I am powerless
to evict you

True Love

true love gives
without promise
of return

Childhood Dreams

you believe beauty is the face
you wore in your youth
that what you have done
is what you are worth
but older is how I know you
with white flecks in your hair
and lines beside tired eyes
what about you I most love
was never how you looked
or what you have accomplished
it is that I heard your heart
beating in my childhood dreams

The Unpaved Path

I am the unpaved path.
The one full of
berries and flowers,
and tangled runaway vines.
I am not the easy option.
Someone who will fit
squarely inside a box.
But I am the one who
would swim oceans for you.
The one who will love you
at dawn and dusk,
and every season that comes.
I have seen down our road.
I see fire, ice, and fertile
blossoming grounds,
that deeply feel like home.
But mostly I see happiness.
I see that as clearly
as I saw my son
inside his father's eyes.

My Son

you are poetry
made with love

Silken Moments

I curved
with the hours
as they bent
me backwards
into the gloaming
of remembrance
and silken
moments
when you were I
and I was you
one breath
between
two people.

The One

the search
could have
stopped
with you

Earth Angel

It was like fireworks,
when he took my hand.
I can still feel it.
And his shoulders, and eyes.
Such deep eyes,
like earth, and wood, and fire.
He is tall, and strong,
and sturdy seeming.
A little animalistic.
His emotions surge
through the atmosphere,
like a lightning
you want to strike you.
Dark hair and eyes.
Handsome, and sexy.
He was elemental.
Energy, synergy. Heat.
So much passion.
He is soft, too, though.
This perfect combination
of strong and soft.
I like that I met him older,
he has gotten better with age,
but I would have
been attracted to him always.
And, mostly, for what
I saw inside of him.
With him, my heart felt home.

Eyes Made of Lava

I fell in love with your flaws first,
and then those eyes made of lava.

Making Love to the Universe

I could have grown old
with our first kiss.
Being with you,
was like,
making love
to the Universe.

To You

and whenever
my mind wanders,
it is always
to you.

Synesthesia

you kissed me
and I could taste music

You Got My Heart

You took my hand,
but got my heart.

Without End

In a world full of endings,
my love will not be one.

Everywhere My Heart Goes

Ducks swim in circles
in a harbor full of boats,
as sunsets fill
old trees with light,
and I think of you.
Then, there, everywhere
my heart goes.
Whether I am alone,
or in a busy room,
during morning,
noon and night,
you are here with me,
a part of every moment.

I Hope to Find You

around the corner,
of every second,
I hope to find you.

So Much

so much of who I am
is who we were

Cherish the people you love the most.
Tell them they are special, loved,
that because of them life is better.
Give them time, kindness, and attention.
Treat them to the best of yourself,
while never taking them for granted.
We only get a few per lifetime,
people whose love is always there,
and tomorrow offers no guarantees.

Branches of the Same Tree

We sat together
in an open meadow
of privet and fluffed grass,
unrushed by the day.
We have always
let each other bloom
in our own time, and way,
like two branches
of the same tree,
and that is what
love should be.
Two people bonded
by the simple things
that forever last.

Through the Lens of My Love

you look beautiful
through the lens
of my love

Family

where others say goodbye,
family says hello.

Vicky

Inside my heart
you will always be,
when the flowers
bloom in Spring,
and whenever purple
coats the air,
I will think of you
with every radiant green
blade of grass
the color of your eyes,
my love will make sure
you are here still,
never to be forgotten

Love Anyway

All the time,
good people
suffer bad things.
Is that fair? No.
But that is life.
Love anyway.

First Kiss

our first kiss
is still my favorite

Permanent Address

I have had many homes,
but you could have been
the permanent address
of my heart.

Relished

very few things
I have relished
in this life
more than you

Present

I was present with you.
Maybe that is how I knew
I could be with you forever.

The Right Person

With the right person,
everything feels possible.
With the wrong person,
nothing does.

What I Loved Most

Your least favorite
things about yourself,
were some of the things
I most loved about you.

Only One Door

It has to feel right, love.
Like a key
fitting into a lock
for which there is only one door.

A Lifetime of Love

You are my mother.
You are my friend.
You gave me life.
And you are giving me
a lifetime of love.

Fiona

Sometimes,
the person
you are waiting for,
is waiting for you too.

You

I met you,
and it was you,
it had always been you.

No Urge to Run

you pulled me into you,
and you were the only one,
I never wanted to pull away from

To Be Your Mother

You curl into the crook of my arm,
cozying up for a morning cuddle,
and I think about all I want to give you –

days full of outdoor play,
and nights glowing with stories,
a home that smells of food,
and sounds like music
being played by a joyful heart,
that loves to laugh and dance and sing.
I want to give you dirt
under your fingernails,
from digging around in the earth,
a rich foundation of a family,
a love that never leaves your side,
confirming it is okay for you to be you.
I want you to have magic, and holidays,
so many reasons to celebrate life,
for you to feel safe to smile, and cry,
for your time to be soft and gentle.

And even with everything
this big and beautiful world has to offer,
what I always most will want
is to be your mother.

My Parents

If I had not had
the parents I have,
I would not be
the person I am.
My life is mine,
because of them.

Love Holds On

love holds on
when everything else
lets go

In the Long Ago

and when you are an old man,
wondering about your decisions,
know that somewhere in the long ago,
someone wanted to choose you.

Some Men Do Stay

You value family,
you are generous,
and steadfast,
and you have taught me
that some men do stay.

Give Out Love

give out all the love
you wish to get,
and in one form or another,
it will come back to you.

Us

It was just us,
as so many times
before it had been.
The sky fell low,
wrapping in fog
turkey vultures
and loping manatees,
but the mangroves
knotted by time
stood wild.
The new year
slid into view,
beckoning us closer,
like a siren
atop a jagged perch.
Together we had
walked so far,
that with your hand
in mine
I felt no worry
or need
for resolution.
I had you
and that
was quite enough.

Half Our Lives

half our lives
we were there
for each other,
so all my life
I will love you

Another Word for Love

Mother
is another word
for love.

Nanny

Some people are loud,
but you were soft,
you radiated gentleness,
and let me feel safe
to hear the song
of my tender heart.

The Heart of a Child

I watch you watch life,
feel the pages of a book
against your cheek, take
a bite of a strawberry,
open a closed door, to
dance barefoot on carpet,
under a sky pouring with rain.
You are so new and tender,
you still believe in the moon,
and the power of a group hug
and I hope you never stop
seeing life with the heart
of a child.

Rainbow Eyes

I love how your eyes
are the color
of everyone
I have ever loved.

Fire in Our Bones

Love is not meant
to be lukewarm,
or fizzle like
a temporary flame,
especially for
those of us born
with fire in our bones.

The Stars in Your Eyes

By the stars
in your eyes,
I could map
the course
of my entire life.

A Lasting Touch

I saw it in your eyes,
and felt it when I held you,
how you trembled with hope,
for a lasting touch.

Lost Poetry

our love lives forever
in the land of lost poetry

What Love Can Be

had you not been born,
I would not have learned
what love can be.

My Life Was Missing You

You were born on this day,
but the gift is mine.
I never knew joy could be a face,
that a morning could bring
the kind of promise it does
when you are with me.
My life was missing you,
you are what I prayed for.
I will never take for granted
one moment of our journey.

The Reason

and should you one day ask me
what the reason is for life,
what is worth the suffering,
and why we all are born,
I will answer only for myself,
that yes there are trees,
there is music, the sweet
and symbolic symphony of words,
that so defines my life,
there are tea sandwiches
eaten where the oleander grow,
there are bedtime stories,
the embrace of long awaiting lovers,
there are family meals and fairy tales,
forests full of flowers
and jungles made of dreams,
but you, my child, you are
the reason for my every step.

Half of You

How could I
not love you,
when he is
half of you?

Strangers With Familiar Eyes

Should we ever meet again,
as strangers with familiar eyes,
I would ask you to come in,
and this time stay forever.

Perfect Fit

I love the way
your soul
fits with mine.

Nature Never Forgets

Nature never forgets.
It remembers
all the seasons,
in seeds below
heavy hills of snow,
and summer flowers
the color of fall leaves.
What rots will bloom.
What rises, falls.
There is no tomorrow
without yesterday.
No ancient tree
whose trunk was not
once at mercy
to the wind.
Wings and roots
will ever be entwined,
as we are for each other,
me holding you
like a bee
holds a petal,
and you holding me,
as the moon
holds the night.

Stronger Than Love

you make me wish
for a word stronger than love
to describe what I feel for you

Holding Hearts

our hearts hold
certain people
the way space
holds the earth

His eyes will be like art, the kind that makes
you stop for hours, studying every stroke. His
soul will feel like a home that never locks its
door. He will feel things, deep within his bones.
He will hear the echo of creation, that beautiful,
haunting cry, and with his hands he will mold
it into something new. He will be open, even when
it hurts, and with me, even when we are apart.
He will reach out. He will believe. He will trust
there is still a little magic left. When we kiss,
I will taste the thunder of his heart, and his
thoughts will strike me like lightning in the
sand. No line will divide us, not when our bodies
blend, or our fears stand watch. He will be my
shelter. He will make me laugh. I will be his
wish, and he will be mine, and we will be love.

Deeper Than These Words

I have been waiting
for something, someone,
faces I thought I knew,
but maybe it was you,
you whose hand I
have never touched,
who touches a part of me
deeper than these words

The Fingerprint of Destiny

Sometimes, the heart just knows.
I have spent years writing these tiny love poems
because I felt the fingerprint of destiny,
deep within my heart.

The Color of Forever

your eyes
were the color
of forever

For You

if the sky
is the limit,
for you,
I could have
given the stars

In the Morning Light

in the morning light,
a record plays,
we gather purple beans
from the garden we have planted,
you read a story,
we give big hugs,
I say "I love you,"
you say "I'm happy."

A Part of Me

a part of me
I didn't even know
existed, began
the day I met you.

Gifts From My Mother

Forever.
Completely.
Love.
Magic.
Home.
Family.
Mother.
Just some of the words
I know the meaning of
because you exist.

Where You Will Stay

you are in my heart
and that is where
you will stay

On a Day Like Today

We met on a day like today
that was cool but also warm,
but our souls needed no introduction,
they have known each other a very long time.
Is it just that we want different things?
Or does the certainty of my love terrify you?

Words That Can Be Scary to Say

"I love you."
"I want you."
"Be with me."

Will We Ever Be

I wonder if you will stay always a fantasy,
somebody I see only in my dreams.
Will we ever again be close enough
for me to feel your heartbeat against my skin?
In your eyes, would I still see my future?
In your arms, would I feel still like I belong?

Our Shot

what I most
wanted with you
was our shot

My Love Will Hold You

you bang your head
your tummy aches
and it is my head
it is my stomach
that hurt as well
my darling child
I will never abandon you
my heart is your
eternal womb
and even when
from this body
my soul departs
my love will hold you

Wishing for More

and one lifetime
hardly feels enough
to love you

Everything

all I ever
wanted with you
was everything

we never know whose lives we most will touch.
it only takes a second to imprint on eternity.
but once that happens, everything is changed.
for me, there is before you, and after,
and the very fact that you were born is the reason
that many of the best things I have are mine.
so today, and every day, I will be grateful,
from my toes to my soul, that you exist.

Some Things Last

Not all things end in smoke,
bellicose desires
venturing into ash.
Some things last.
Like sunshine
high above the clouds,
and ocean mist
on tender mornings.
In this sea of infinity,
that binds us
between life and death,
love can last as well.
Anchor to my heart,
and you will never
drift away.

Soulful Eyes

your soulful eyes
stare into my dreams,
windows to a time
when I knew for sure
who I was meant for

What Defines Us Most

We are so fragile,
stitched together
with such delicate thread.
A pair of blue eyes,
a worn set of hands,
a reel of old memories,
a heart that daily beats
the sound of new hope.
This is all we have,
as we tread water
through time,
these tender parts,
that shape us into form.
But what defines us most,
is the love we give each other.

A Star Above

my love,
when I am but
a star above,
know my heart
still will beat
for you

The Goodness There

all of you I saw
you are arrogant
and selfish
using girls like pills
to numb the pain
afraid someone real
could hold you
longer than a night
you detach first
breaking the hold
that binds you
with most people
and any who stay
you show only pieces
of who you are
all of you I saw
and your faults
could not conceal
the goodness there
you hide the shy boy
you think weakens you
but his sweet face
will always stand you out
in a crowd of four billion

One Cosmic Heart

What if our lips never meet?
What if we grow old apart?
What if you always are there,
and I always am here,
two halves of one cosmic heart?
What if it all works out?

Soul Knowing

and when it is
the soul that knows,
there is no use
trying to talk sense
into the mind

The Wish

You were the wish
I told myself
not to want too much
because wishes
rarely come true,
and yet you did.

A Little Bit in Love

wild chicken feathers
oily with dawn light
swept into my calves
and the lagoon
glistened green
I gathered leisurely
a steamy baguette
cold island water
a scoop of fresh jam
and next to an old palm
bending slightly
under the weight of its years
with pen and paper sat
I saw you there
a stranger and artist
forgotten by those
who once had loved you
eyes brown as singed wood
skin showered with sunshine
your hair long
like my native ancestors
you spoke no words
that center pensione table
was your address
in this world
that so easily abandons
your only possessions
charcoal and paper
into which you scratched eyes
with stained black fingers
a thousand circles
a billion
one at least
you needed to see you
and confirm you exist
not knowing there I was
a little bit in love
and a lifetime inspired

Protection

My love
is strong enough
to protect you.

Your Eyes Told Me

your eyes
told me
all the stories
you have never
shared with
anyone

It all sounds good. Nights in and days out.
Being wrapped in passion so complete we are
uncertain where one of us ends and the other
begins. I want lots and lots of that. Filling
albums with the memories that make us a family.
Even the arguments. I want a wedding with
vows, the kind that never break, not even
from the pressure of our worst days together.
I want the smiles. I want the tears. But
maybe what I want most of all, is to be the
person sitting next to you during the 3am
emergency hospital visit, because you have
a sore throat, or even if your heart aches.
I want the no matter what, I am not going
anywhere, I am in this for the good times,
and the bad, take my hand, kind of love.

Our Hearts

Our hearts
can't help
who they
beat for.

In Love

In love,
there is no better,
without the worse.

Your Light

And if you ever question
how bright your light is,
think of the lighthouse
in a perfect storm,
or the North Star
guiding people home.

And When

and when the snow falls,
and the moon signals night,
and the trees sing with birds,
and the hours fill with light,
I think of you

Distant Ports

We are different now,
with all this time between us.
Once, we shared a horizon,
but now we are like ships
with seas too vast to cross,
docked at distant ports.
Yet, for the waves we rode as one,
the sunsets and rises only our eyes saw,
my heart will ever hold you.

Fire or Honey

I wonder what
it would be like
to kiss you,
would you taste
of fire, or honey,
would I feel
at home in your arms,
will I ever know?

I Dream of You

I dream of you
in sunlight,
not only
when the moon
shows your face

The Woman You Are

if I am a fraction
of the woman you are,
and the mother
you have been to me,
I will be lucky

Mama and Baby

I nuzzle the soft skin
on your forehead
while you drink
your morning meal
your rainbow eyes
taking me in
you point
the musical jellyfish
pictures on the wall
my adoring face
I see you already
becoming when
this time last year
you were still
inside me

Connected

It feels still like
we are connected

could the moon
ever exist
without the sun

like when you
breathe in
it is my exhale
that follows

when you are sad
your tears
roll down my cheeks

and when my heart
beats, it is your
echo I feel inside

Like Rain

you were like rain
on soil
that had
never been watered

People Are the Gift

Nothing that comes with a bow
will ever be better
than the person giving it.

In Relationships

There should be laughter,
and kisses,
and comfort.

My Child

I look at your face
and I see everything
that has gone right
in my life.

Be My Eternity

I never wanted us
to be a time and a place.
I wanted you
to be my eternity.

Spiralled Into One

love shares of itself,
with time and trust,
it is inclusive,
a tender and safe
weaving of people,
like trees across seasons,
whose branches and trunks,
have spiralled into one

All You Are

You are
My season
My reason
My lifetime

A Love Like I Have Never Known

I hope each day
a knock will come
from love
upon my door.

But if love comes
again my way
this time
it must be naked.

I need the body,
heart, and mind,
the soul to be
exposed.

Bare of secrets,
stripped of lies,
a love like I
have never known.

It Just Is

My love for you
does not depend
on a return.
It just is
and will always be.

Filled With Heart

she held him closer
than anyone before
as he painted the world
he was going to give her
the walls and door
that opened a home
built with wood
but filled with heart
and the family
their love created

Some People Are the Poem

some people
are the poem,
like dewdrops
in morning grass,
and breathing in
warm air
that echoes
of mermaids
in a summer sea.
your hair,
that once was black
as a bird's wing,
has lightened now,
but your heart
stays young
as a flower
opening petals
for the first time.
you teach me grace,
you show me kindness,
you give me song.
you are the friend
I always want to call,
but you also
are my mother,
and my greatest
source of love.

My Heart Answers

when they ask
how I know,
my heart answers
because I do

Naked

I am naked
in front of you,
more than I
ever was before.
All my pages
you have read,
and you have not
turned away,
even when my words
bit hard into you,
leaving marks.
I see you too,
without anything on.
In the shadows
you are there,
a heavenly ray
of pulsing light,
illuminating infinity.

Like Prophecy

Your touch
was like prophecy,

your eyes a warm
and endless sky.

You are the height
of my daydreams,

your heart the key
to my locked chamber.

You spun me into you
with your hands,

but it was the harmony
of our shared song

that made me yours.

To Dance

Love will
ask you
to the dance.

The One I Want

yours are the arms
I want to hold me.
you are the one
I want to be with.

Centering Prayer

in the darkness
your heart beat
a centering prayer
and call to life
that still guides me
which paths to follow

Unmasked Love

No matter how many
faces you wear,
the right person
still will love you

The Harvest

Maybe he was the harvest,
a season to bring
sweet fruit into my life,
but he felt to me
more ancient and lasting.
Imagine standing
in the gloaming,
shore birds singing
lullabies to the night.
The waves collide,
salt landing on your lips,
and underneath
an infinite horizon,
the sand is hot.
The sun is there too,
dressed in persimmon,
cherry, and a yellow
so buttery it smoothly
spreads across the sky.
You feel deep peace
and complete presence,
in that sacred spot,
that smells of creation.
You know that somewhere
in the stream of time,
you have been here before,
as will you be here again.
That is why you feel you know.
Sometimes every road
we will ever take
leads us to one destination.
And once we are there
the heart simply knows
there is nowhere else
we are meant to be.

A Lifetime of Poetry

you inspired
in one moment
a lifetime of poetry
inside my heart

Your Colors

Time winds like a river
never reaching the sea,
and on either side
are memories I can see
but not quite touch.
Your colors painted
grey out of my world,
and into my heart eternity.
I float like a dream that
cannot anchor to night,
unsure what is right,
if I am wrong about you.

The Words in My Heart

You are
the words
in my heart,
and every time
I try to write
about anything else,
these letters
lead me
back to you.

Echo

you echo
across
canyons
of time

He took my heart by surprise.
Eyes bursts of blazing umber,
he smelled of water and wood,
and deep violet wishes
sunk by wells.
His hands were rough
like the skin of the trees
I used to hide in as a girl,
and when he said "Hello,"
I could have said "I do."

Safety

Love is
safety
to share
all our colors.

No Match

Hate is
no match
for a heart
strong with love.

Enough

some people
are enough
in such a way
that even in absence
no one else compares

Thinking About Them

thinking about them
should make
your heart
smile

The Wave

you are the wave
I could ride
forever

Stay

see me
for all I am
and all I am not
and stay

Song Without Words

Love is a song
without words
played
by the heart

A Union of Souls

Love is
a union
of souls
unbound
by time,
a tapestry
of emotion
and experience.

Prisms of Possibility

The way water
mixes with light
to create prisms
of possibility,
that was how we were.

Without Our Permission

Love is a choice
our hearts make
without our permission

Only We

only me,
only you,
only we
could make beauty
like this

In One Motion

your fingers wrapped
around mine, like your body,
me spun in one motion
away from past, and into present.
a canal of longing
surged into my heart
and into my future you flowed.

Whole

The rain fell for hours
that felt like minutes,
and you were finally closer
than you had ever been
in my dreams, I whole
in your embrace, no want
for anything but you.

Soft Ears

I rub your soft ears,
during gentle morning moments,
remembering the night
I first held you in my arms.
This love is beyond words,
it is more than moments,
and beautiful memories
that only we can make.
I look at you and finally see.
You are every why and step.
The only question I have
is what I did to deserve you.

Shining Only for You

there are stars
in my heart
shining only
for you

Perfection

Maybe,
it is so hard to let go,
because being with you,
is about as close as I have come
to experiencing perfection.

I Need

I need to be held
by arms as strong
as old branches,
somewhere without time.

I need to be kissed
like rain upon dry earth,
until I feel the river
running through me.

I need a night
that does not end
with morning,
and a day
that never
fades away.

I need you
holding me
holding you
where angels
dress like stars.

Some Things Make Sense

Like Chopin's Nocturne in B Minor,
and the smell of grass after the rain,
some things make sense, and will,
like the people we most love,
become a part of our hearts,
offering, in simple, gentle ways,
that grace the surface of today,
harmony and a happiness to hold on to.

Flowers to the Sun

Let us open
to each other
like flowers
to the sun.

October Day

that was the day
the poetry began

With My Heart

my eyes
have always
been open,
but I see best
with my heart

Like Winter Branches

Give me a love
like winter branches,
that will hold on
even without
any leaves.

The Wisdom of the Trees

I wonder how long
you have turned inwards
towards each other?
How many seasons
of snowflakes,
and sunshine,
and tiny white flowers
safely tucked into spring?
How many branches
have broken off
between you?
How often have you
needed to show forgiveness?
As often as the rain?
Or only when the
belted kingfisher glides
in on a wind directed
by the harvest moon?
What heart holds you
for the stars,
on empty nights,
when they cannot be seen?
If I come to you,
put my hand on your bark,
penitent and resigned,
will you teach me
the wisdom of the trees?

Heart Springs

love
is keeping
within the heart,
an indomitable
and ever blooming
spring

How You Came to Be

and when you
ask me
how you
came to be,
I will tell you
about magic
and a love
that lasts

I Wish You

I wish you fireflies,
and places to wander,
where your feet can run bare
through open fields of grass,
I wish you a heart
that always hears the music,
and a dance floor
wherever you choose to go,
I wish you family, and freedom,
a moon and a sun
that never cease to shine,
I wish you tenderness,
and resilience,
passion and learning,
a lifetime hopefully full more
of smiles than frowns,
I wish you love, and meaning,
comfort, and peace.

Moments Like These

It is the moments with loved ones,
where we are simply
sitting next to them
on the couch –

I don't need to know
any part
of the rest of my journey,

to know my life will be made
by moments like these.

I Will Want You All

if we ever meet,
somewhere between
there and now,
I hope you hold
firmly onto me,
but not back,
any part of yourself,
for I will want you all.

The Journey Back

if only
the journey back
could bring me
to you

Fashioned Old

I was fashioned old.
Bare feet, on hot sand.
Sitting on a wooden bench,
while trees tell me stories
of the days long past.
Dancing to vinyl in the kitchen,
as I stir garden fresh mint,
slowly, into a sauce.
I crave a style of love
like tea steeping in water,
something that comforts
more than my body,
but that fills my cup
with warmth, peace,
and magic.

Another Time

I crave
a style of love
suited for
another time,
when things
were built to last,
and a promise
was a pledge.

Hands

how can one pair of hands,
that aren't even touching me,
fill me with such desire?

Beautiful Dream

how beautiful
a dream
we are

Desire

desire was just a word,
before we met,
without much of a meaning,
but it now defines
every one of my days.

Before Hello

what wouldn't I tell you,
what wouldn't I share,
you who had me before hello,
of myself I would give everything,
and more, if I could

Half of Me

Half of me
is all of you,
so even when
we are apart
we are together.

My Father

On a one-way street,
you taught me
how to ride a bike.
And one weekend,
when the air
was tropical,
a line of salty blue
flattened a horizon
that looked like
it had never seen
a single storm,
so we could become
the best of friends.
We share nebulae,
and misfit films,
a love of Halloween,
and herb gardens.
In waterfalls of
Canadian Centurea
I see you, and as
a hushed voice,
I hear you wishing
Grandpa more time.
You speak more in silence
than you do with words,
but the half of me
that is all of you,
translates who you are
into the purest expression
of unbroken love.

So much is inherited. We all are half both our parents, which even when times are hard, is a nice thought. For me, for them, for my son. Wherever and whenever I am, my father and my mother are with me, in my entire being. The musical theater my mother loves, the fascination with stars held by my father. Our history, genetic, and sociological. Things told and untold. They are not only always in my heart, but in everything that makes me who I am. All my choices, and experiences.

Families, all, are complicated webs of emotion and experience. Things rarely are smooth. And sometimes our greatest pain is rooted in where we come from, as one friend has shared, about her experience. But for me, and maybe you, family is that eternal why. I look in my father's blue eyes, I hold my mother's hand, and I see everything. An ancient story of love, that began long before this time.

My son and I were talking about his father a few weeks back, he asks me a lot of questions suited for an older child, and I said what I always say. How his father saved my heart, and made my wish come true, and how he is someone I always will love. From his car seat, he said how he loves his father too. And I felt proud. Proud he feels love how he does. Proud of who he is. Proud of myself, and my family, as did I feel lucky. For all of our flaws, we are a loving bunch of people, who truly care about each other, even when we struggle to show it, and hopefully, at least a little, these words show my eternal love for these people who matter to me as much as my breath.

If I Was a Tree

If I was a tree,
would you come close,
would you take me
in your hands,
wrap your arms
around my bark,
would you spread
me out beneath you,
smoothing out
all my lines,
would you shape me
into something
even more beautiful
than I already am

A Home Outside Space

love should be
soft, sturdy,
a place to
relinquish fear,
a home
outside space

Because of You

I know what love is,
because of you.

Worship

we are
these moments
right here.

let's worship them.

We Are These Moments

we are these moments
right here,
going for a walk
on a day
where the mud
smells like spring,
sharing with a neighbor,
watching our child
climb an old pile of snow.
we gather treasure
when time
cannot be found
on a clock,
when we are with others
who love us,
when we are free,
and wild.

A Gift

to even
be able
to dream
is a gift

The Memory of Water

the memory
of water,
keeps me
reaching
for rain